dabblelab

CIRCUIT CREATIONS 4D

MAKE ART WITH CIRCUITS

4D AN AUGMENTED READING EXPERIENCE

by Chris Harbo and Sarah L. Schuette

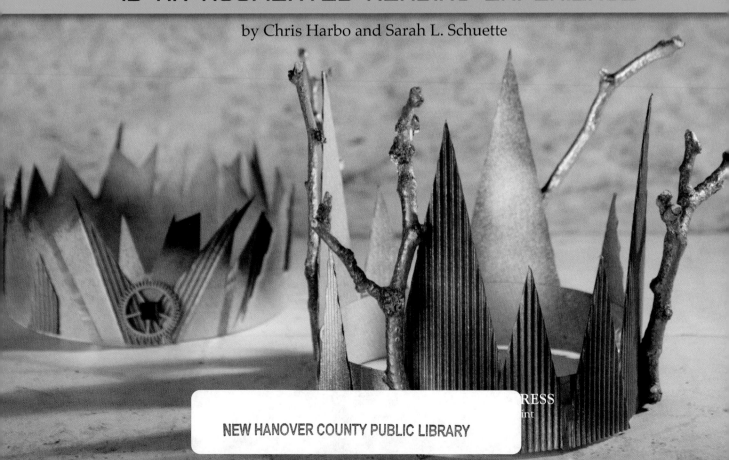

RESS
int

Dabble Lab is published by Capstone Press,
1710 Roe Crest Drive, North Mankato, Minnesota 56003
www.capstonepub.com

Library of Congress Cataloging-in-Publication Data
Names: Harbo, Christopher L., author. | Schuette, Sarah L., author.
Title: Make art with circuits / by Chris Harbo and
    Sarah L. Schuette.
Description: First edition. | North Mankato, Minnesota : Capstone
    Press, [2020] | Series: Dabble lab. Circuit creations 4D | Series: 4D,
    an augmented reading experience | Audience: Age 8-10. | Audience:
    Grades 4 to 6.
Identifiers: LCCN 2019008534| ISBN 9781543539882 (hardcover) | ISBN
    9781543539929 (paperback) | ISBN 9781543539967 (eBook pdf)
Subjects: LCSH: Electronic circuits--Juvenile literature. | Electronic
    toys—Juvenile literature. | Handicraft—Juvenile literature.
Classification: LCC TK9971 .H37 2020 | DDC 745.5—dc23
LC record available at https://lccn.loc.gov/2019008534

Editorial Credits
Abby Colich, editor; Juliette Peters, designer; Jo Miller, media researcher;
Laura Manthe, production assistant

Photo Credits
All photographs by Capstone: Karon Dubke; Marcy Morin and Sarah Schuette,
Project Production; Heidi Thompson, Art Director

Design Elements:
Capstone; Shutterstock: bygermina, rikkyall

All internet sites appearing in back matter were available and accurate when
this book was sent to press.

Printed in the United States of America.
PA70

Download the Capstone 4D app!

- Ask an adult to download the Capstone 4D app.

- Scan the cover and stars inside the book for additional content.

When you scan a spread, you'll find
fun extra stuff to go with this book!
You can also find these things
on the web at www.capstone4D.com
using the password: art.39882

TABLE OF CONTENTS

● ● ● ● ●

Circuits that Shine 4

What Is a Circuit? 6

Simple Circuits 8

    Light-Up Party Invitations 10

    Light-Up Gift Tag 12

    Robot Masks 14

    Musical Thank You Cards 16

    Holiday Train Station 18

    Glowing Origami Clock 22

Simple Conductor Circuits 26

    Canvas Art 28

    Crown Centerpieces 30

Salt and Dough Circuits 32

    Glowing Dough Camp Scene 36

Moving Circuits 38

    Animated Art Bots 40

    Spinning Wire Art 42

    Giraffe Diorama 44

Glossary 46

Read More 47

Internet Sites 47

CIRCUITS THAT SHINE

From festive lights to dancing robots, everything that uses electricity to glow or move relies on a circuit. And even though circuits may seem complicated, they really aren't. With a few inexpensive materials, you can make several safe and simple circuits yourself. But that's not all. You can also use these circuits to add pizzazz to your art projects. From spinning wire art and light-up gift tags to glowing paintings and animated art bots, the power of circuits will make your artwork shine!

SAFETY TIPS

While working with circuits and electricity, keep these important safety tips in mind.

- All projects should be done with adult supervision.

- Always disconnect your circuits when not in use.

- Never put batteries in your mouth.

- Never experiment with outlets in the wall.

WHAT IS A CIRCUIT?

In its simplest form, a circuit is a looping path that an electric current flows through. For this path to carry electricity, it often uses four main components. These are a power source, a conductor, a load, and a controller.

Common power sources for circuits are batteries and wall outlets. A conductor is any material, such as metal wire, that can carry electricity. A load is a device, such as a light bulb or motor, that uses the electricity to work. And a controller is a switch that starts or stops the flow of electricity.

For any circuit to work, all four components must be connected in an unbroken loop. When you turn on a flashlight's switch, a closed circuit is created. Electricity flows from the battery, along a wire, through the switch, to the light bulb, and back to the battery. When you flick the flashlight's switch off, a break in the circuit stops the flow of electricity to turn the light bulb off.

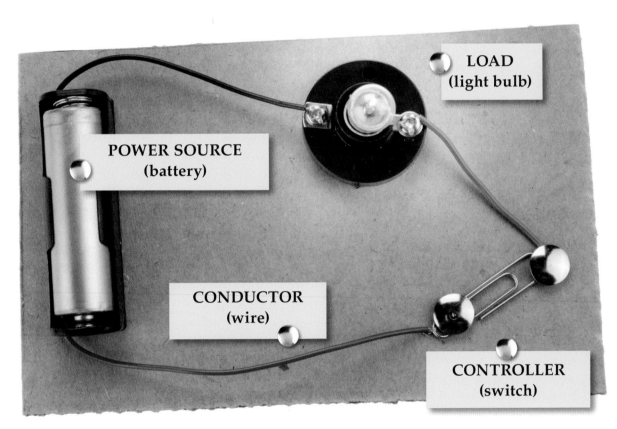

LOAD
(light bulb)

POWER SOURCE
(battery)

CONDUCTOR
(wire)

CONTROLLER
(switch)

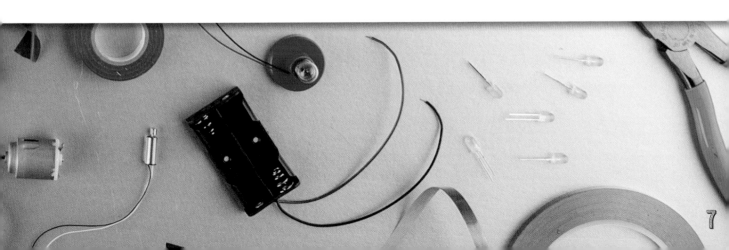

SIMPLE CIRCUITS

Now that you know how circuits work, you can practice connecting them. Then use your imagination to add circuits to common objects and create new things. You can make circuits with a variety of batteries, bulbs, and other easy-to-find items. Use what you have available.

WHAT YOU NEED

AA battery in holder with lead wires
bulb socket and bulb
small screwdriver
insulated wire
wire stripper
2 metal thumbtacks
cardboard
metal paper clip
LED
CR2032 button battery
electrical tape

MAKE IT! ●●●○○

LIGHT UP A LIGHT BULB

1. Connect the black wire from the battery holder to one side of the light bulb socket. If the socket has screws, use them to hold the wire in place.

2. Repeat with the red wire and the other side of the socket. The light bulb will light up!

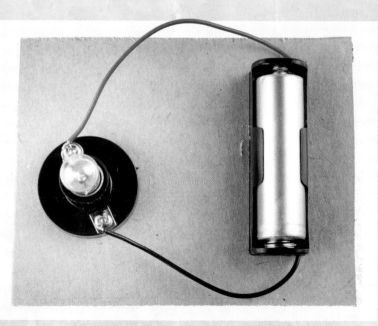

ADD A SWITCH

1. Connect the black wire from the battery holder to one side of the light bulb socket.

2. Cut a piece of wire. Use the wire stripper to strip both ends. Connect one end of the wire to the open side of the socket. Wrap the other end of the wire around a thumbtack. Press the thumbtack into the cardboard.

3. Connect the red wire from the battery holder to the end of a metal paper clip. Press the second thumbtack through the paper clip and into the cardboard. This thumbtack should be a short distance from the first thumbtack.

4. Move the paper clip to open and close the circuit and turn the light bulb on and off.

LIGHT UP AN LED

1. Slide an LED bulb onto a button battery. The long leg should touch the positive (+) side of the battery. The short leg should touch the negative (-) side.

2. Wrap electrical tape around the battery to hold the LED in place.

TIP!

Cut a small piece from a plastic lid. Slide it under an LED leg to turn the light off. Remove it to turn it back on.

STRIPPING WIRES

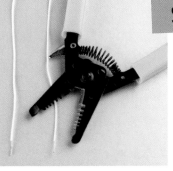

Before you begin making circuits, practice stripping wires. To strip, or remove the coating on the end of a wire, use a wire stripper. Line up the wire size with the same size hole on the stripper. Press down lightly to cut into the coating without cutting the wire. Then pull the stripper away from your body.

LIGHT-UP PARTY INVITATIONS

Share your circuit-building skills with your friends. Invite them to a party with light-up invitations.

WHAT YOU NEED

scissors
cardstock
craft supplies
2 LEDs
2 CR2032 button batteries
electrical tape
pen or marker

MAKE IT!

1. Cut a piece of cardstock to your desired size and fold it in half. Decorate the front of the card with craft supplies and plan out where the light will go.

2. Open the card and push the legs of the LEDs through the front of it.

3. Slide a button battery between the legs of each LED. The long legs should be on the positive (+) side of the batteries and the short legs on the negative (-) side.

4. Secure the LED legs to the button batteries with electrical tape.

5. Use a pen or marker to write the date, time, and place for the party on the inside of the invitation.

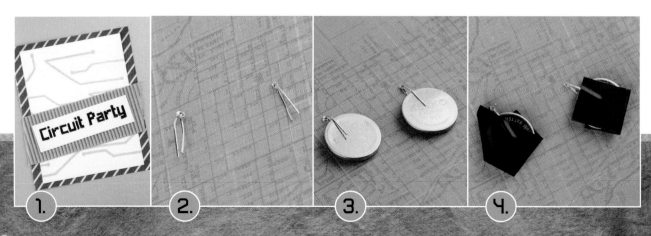

1. 2. 3. 4.

LIGHT-UP GIFT TAG

Gift giving isn't just about what's inside the box. Design your own gift tags that add a touch of pizzazz to your presents!

WHAT YOU NEED

cardstock
CR2032 button batteries
LEDs
electrical tape
twine or string
hole punch

MAKE IT!

1. Cut a tag shape out of cardstock. Plan where you want the lights on the front.

2. Push the legs of the LEDs through the cardstock.

3. Slide a button battery between the legs of each LED. The long legs should be on the positive (+) side of the batteries and the short legs on the negative (-) side.

4. Secure the LED legs to the button batteries with electrical tape.

5. Punch a hole in the tag and thread a piece of twine through the hole.

6. Attach the tag to a gift and connect it right before you give the gift.

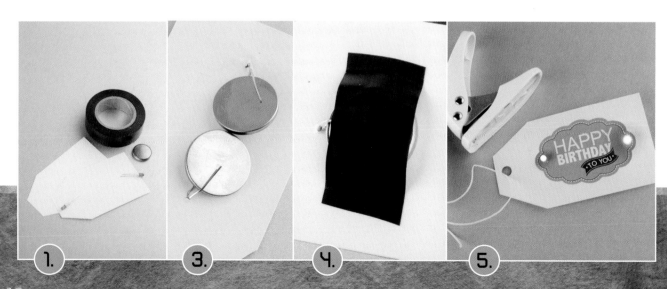

1.   3.   4.   5.

CHANGE IT UP!

Use scrapbook paper, patterned tape, and stickers to decorate the tag. Write names or greetings with a marker.

GIFT GIVING!

Being generous is one way to show people you care about them. Use these fun tags to give thank you gifts, birthday gifts, or just give gifts for fun. Add light-up cards and make personalized artwork. Gifts don't have to be something you buy. Some of the best gifts are homemade!

ROBOT MASKS

Get into gear for your next costume party. These clever robot masks not only hide your face, but also show off your engineering skills.

WHAT YOU NEED

- scissors
- cardboard
- hot glue gun
- large craft stick
- paint
- markers
- circuit and craft scraps
- light bulb and socket
- AA battery holder with lead wires
- small screwdriver
- AA battery

MAKE IT!

1. Cut a rectangle out of the cardboard that's large enough to cover your face. Cut notches around the edges of the rectangle to make it look like a gear.

2. Hot glue a large craft stick to the bottom of the cardboard mask.

3. Decorate your mask with paint, markers, and circuit and craft scraps.

4. Glue the light bulb socket and the battery holder to the mask.

5. Use a small screwdriver to connect the black wire from the battery holder to one side of the light bulb socket. Repeat with the red wire and the other side of the socket. Then place a battery in the holder.

2.   4.   5.

DECORATE IT!

Don't hold back when it comes to decorating your mask. Add mesh, nuts, bolts, tubing, or gears. You can even experiment with other types of circuits found in this book to add more extras to your mask.

TIP!

If your robot mask gets heavy, just add another large craft stick for stability. You can simply wrap them together with duct tape.

MUSICAL THANK YOU CARDS

A little gratitude goes a long way. After a party, send musical cards to thank your friends and family for coming.

WHAT YOU NEED

scissors
cardstock
craft supplies
markers
music button with lead wires
craft glue
electrical tape

MAKE IT!

1. Cut a piece of cardstock to your desired size and fold it in half. Use markers and miscellaneous craft scraps to write "thank you" and decorate the front of the card in any way you like.

2. Connect one wire of the music button to the positive (+) side of a button battery. Connect the other wire to the negative (-) side of the battery. Wrap the connected battery with electrical tape.

3. Glue a music button circuit onto the inside flap of the card. Let dry.

4. Cut another piece of cardstock the same size as the inside flap of the card. Make and glue a circular "Press" sign to the piece of cardstock.

5. Glue the piece of cardstock over the top of the music button circuit to hide it. Let dry. When the "Press" sign is pushed, the music button will activate.

6. Write a note inside the card that thanks people for coming to your party.

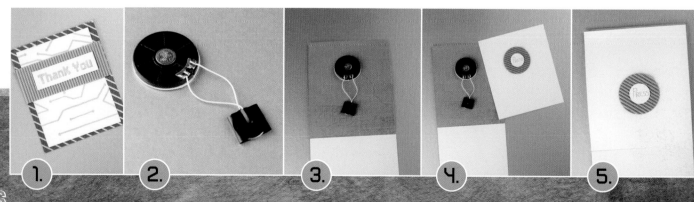

1.   2.   3.   4.   5.

Thank You

TIP!

Many greeting cards have music buttons built into them. If you get one for your birthday, save it! You can remove the music buttons and reuse them in your circuit projects. You can also buy music buttons in the doll section of most craft stores.

HOLIDAY TRAIN STATION

All aboard! Brighten up the holidays with a train station, train, and city skyline that casts a festive glow.

WHAT YOU NEED

scissors or craft knife
assorted boxes
clear tape
wax paper
paint and paintbrushes
plastic packaging scraps
craft glue
wood skewer
LEDs
CR2032 button batteries
electrical tape
cardboard

MAKE IT!

TRAINS

1. Cut holes along the sides of long, narrow boxes to make train windows. Tape wax paper over the windows on the insides of the boxes.

2. Paint plastic packaging scraps. Once dry, glue them to the tops of the trains.

3. Use a wood skewer to punch two holes in the end of each box. Push LEDs into the holes.

4. Open the box flaps with the LEDs and slide button batteries between the LED legs. The long legs should touch the positive (+) sides, and the short legs should touch the negative (-) sides of the batteries.

5. Wrap the LED button battery circuits with electrical tape, and then close the box flaps.

6. Make two more LED button battery circuits. Open the back end of each train, place a button battery inside each end, and close the flaps. The windows of your trains will light up.

TRAIN STATION TICKET BOOTH AND WAITING AREA

1. Cut the flaps off one end of a small rectangular box.

2. Cut a hole in the front of the box to make a ticket window. Tape wax paper over the hole on the inside of the box.

3. Paint a plastic packaging piece and, once dry, glue it to the top of the ticket booth as a decoration.

4. Cut windows in a second small box. Tape wax paper on the inside of the windows.

5. Glue the second small box to the side of the ticket booth. Let dry.

6. Cut a cardboard rectangle large enough to hold the ticket booth and waiting room. Set your buildings on the cardboard base.

7. Make two LED button battery circuits. Place them under the ticket booth and waiting room to light them up.

TIP!

Boxes for toothpaste, butter, plastic wrap, crackers, and taco shells are perfect for this craft.

○●○●○○ TURN THE PAGE.

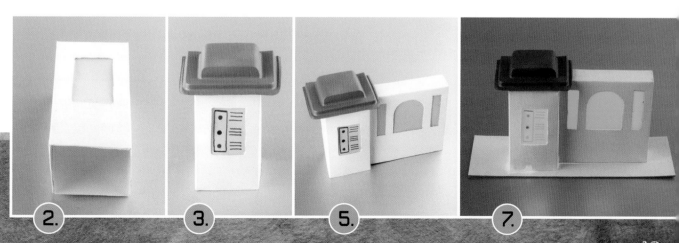

2.   3.   5.   7.

CITY SKYLINE

1. Stand boxes of different sizes together to form a city skyline.

2. Cut a piece of cardboard large enough to hold all of the boxes. Set the boxes on the cardboard base.

3. Use a wood skewer to poke holes in the front of the buildings to make skyscraper windows.

4. Cut larger holes to make office buildings or store fronts. Add wax paper behind all the windows and doors.

5. Make LED button battery circuits and set them inside the boxes to see the city lights twinkle.

TIP!

Go small! Make mini circuit-powered buildings out of tiny boxes. Then just glue on a string to make them into glowing ornaments.

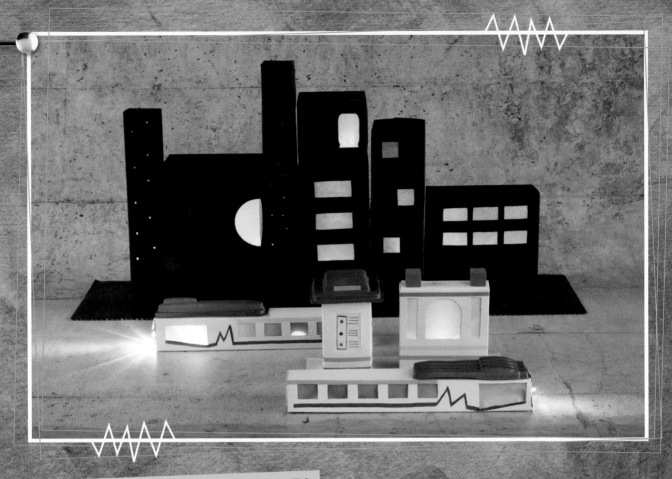

PUT IT ALL TOGETHER!

Once you've created all of the pieces of your train station scene, it's time to put them all together. Start with the city buildings as the backdrop. Then position the trains, ticket booth, and waiting area in front of them. But why stop there? What other circuit-powered parts could you make for this scene? Test your skills by creating wired streetlights or lit-up landmarks.

CHANGE IT UP!

Change your train scene for each season. Add cotton balls for snow. Cut out paper leaves in fall. Add paper cone trees or make city street graphite drawings. Decorate your trains and buildings with markers, tape, or paint.

GLOWING ORIGAMI CLOCK

Showcase a small clock with a simple origami frame. Then add a little backlight to bring out its brilliance.

WHAT YOU NEED

6-inch (15-centimeter) square of paper
36-inch (91-cm) square of paper
scissors
cardboard
hot glue gun
LEDs
CR2032 button batteries
electrical tape
removable adhesive wall mounts
small battery-powered clock

PRACTICE FOLDING IT!

1. Place the 6-inch (15-cm) paper square colored side down on a table. Fold edge to edge and unfold.

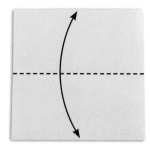

2. Fold the edges to the center.

3. Fold edge to edge and unfold.

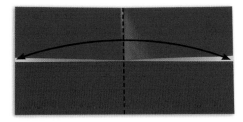

4. Fold the edges to the center and unfold.

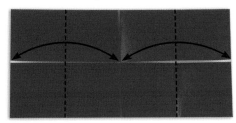

5. Fold the edge to the creases made in step 4 and unfold.

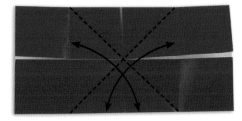

6. Squash the paper using the existing creases.

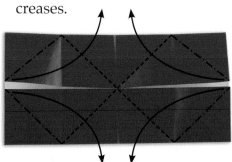

7. Fold the inside edges of each flap to the center.

8. Squash all four points using the existing creases.

9. Fold the edges of each of the four squares to their center creases.

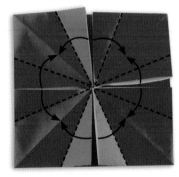

10. Squash all of the triangles.

11. Fold all four points.

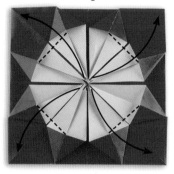

12. Fold all four points.

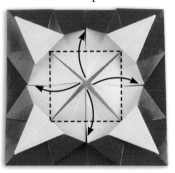

13. Finished origami frame.

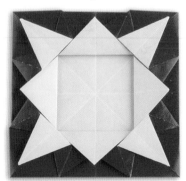

○●○○○● TURN THE PAGE.

MAKE IT! ●●●●●

1. Fold the 36-inch (91-cm) square of paper into an origami frame using the steps on pages 22–23.

2. Cut a piece of cardboard that is slightly smaller than your finished origami frame.

3. Attach the cardboard to the back of the origami frame with hot glue.

4. Slide button batteries between the LED legs. The long legs should touch the positive (+) sides, and the short legs should touch the negative (-) sides of the batteries.

5. Place the button battery circuits behind the paper flaps of the origami frame. Secure the circuits to the frame with electrical tape.

6. Place a battery-powered clock or your favorite photo in the center of the origami frame. Use hot glue to secure it firmly in place.

7. Stick the frame to the wall with removable adhesive wall mounts. Watch how the lights create shadows on the wall. Adjust the lights to change the shadows.

1.   3.   5.

TIP!

You can use just about any kind of paper for this project. Origami paper comes in many colors, patterns, and sizes. It can be found in most craft stores. But many other types of paper can work too. Be creative and experiment with wrapping paper, old maps, or even paper bags to find the look you like best.

SIMPLE CONDUCTOR CIRCUITS

Graphite, copper, foil, and other elements are good conductors for electricity. Electricity can flow through them, and they can be used to make paths for electricity. These paths are called traces. The best way to practice these circuits is on paper. Once you learn the basics, you can experiment with them on other surfaces.

WHAT YOU NEED

graphite pencil (2B or harder)
paper
LEDs
clear tape
9-volt battery
CR2032 button battery
copper tape

MAKE IT! ●●●●●

GRAPHITE CIRCUIT

1. With the graphite pencil, draw two parallel lines. Mark the ends of one line with positive (+) symbols. Then mark the other line with negative (-) symbols.

2. Open the legs of the LED. Tape each leg to one end of your lines. The long leg should touch the line with the positive (+) symbol. The short leg should touch the line with the negative (-) symbol.

3. Set the connection ports of the 9-volt battery on the other end of your lines. Match up the positive and negative ports of the battery to the markings on your drawing.

4. The LED will light up if the circuit is connected correctly. You may need to check the circuit in a dark place. The LED will be dimmer than lights from other circuits.

COPPER TAPE CIRCUIT

1. Use the graphite pencil to sketch a circuit path with two openings.

2. Remove the backing of the copper tape. Stick the copper tape on top of your sketch.

3. Spread the legs of the LED and tape them to the copper tape at one of the circuit's openings. One leg should connect to each end of copper tape.

4. At the second opening, place a button battery on top of one end of the copper tape. Then fold the corner of the paper over so the other end of the copper tape touches the top of the battery. Watch the LED light up.

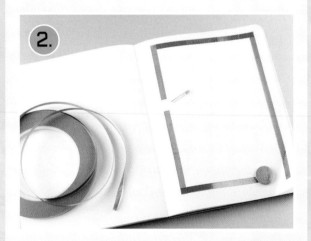

CIRCUIT PENS AND PAINT

Experimenting with circuit writer pens and paint can be a lot of fun. Circuit pens can be found in craft stores. They work by drawing over the top of your graphite sketches. Once your traced lines are dry, just connect a battery and LED and watch the LED light up.

Circuit paint can be made by mixing the same amounts of liquid graphite powder and acrylic paint. Once again, just trace over your graphite circuits with the conductive paint, let it dry, and then hook up your components.

TIP!

Before you use copper tape, cut a small piece and remove the backing. Does the tape look the same on both sides? If it does, then both sides of the tape are conductive. Some copper tape is only conductive on one side. Be very careful with copper tape. The edges can be sharp.

CANVAS ART

How can you bring a simple canvas painting to life? Just use the power of copper tape to light it up!

WHAT YOU NEED

acrylic paint
paintbrush
artist's canvas with wooden frame
pencil
LEDs
CR2032 button battery
copper tape

MAKE IT!

1. Paint a simple scene on the front of an artist's canvas, such as an apple tree with a tire swing. Let dry.

2. Use a pencil to mark spots on the tree where you'd like apples to hang.

3. Poke LED legs through the canvas at the spots marked in step 2. The legs of the LEDs will stick out of the back of the canvas.

4. Bend the LED legs flat on the back of the canvas. Connect all of the long LED legs with one strip of copper tape. Connect one end of this copper strip to the positive (+) side of a button battery.

5. Connect all of the short LED legs with a second strip of copper tape. Attach the end of this copper strip to the negative (-) side of the battery. The LEDs on the front of the canvas will all light up.

6. Turn your glowing canvas over and hang it on the wall.

1.   3.   5.

CHANGE IT UP!

The sky's the limit when it comes to the scenes you can paint and then light up with circuits! Create a nighttime camping scene and let the LEDs light up the fire. Paint a city skyline and use LEDs as streetlights and lit windows. Or really have some fun and paint a flying saucer hovering above Earth. With LEDs on the spacecraft, your artwork will truly be out of this world!

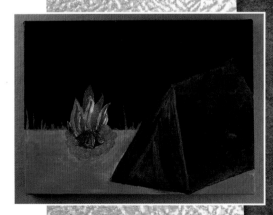

CROWN CENTERPIECES

Give your next party a royal theme. These glowing crowns use copper tape circuits to create a stunning centerpiece for any table.

WHAT YOU NEED

scissors
poster board
cardboard
hot glue gun
paint
paintbrush
copper tape
LEDs
CR2032 button battery

MAKE IT!

1. Cut out a strip of poster board. Then cut a variety of tall triangle shapes out of cardboard.

2. Glue the triangle shapes around the base of the poster board strip to create a crown band. Paint the crown band any way you like.

3. Line the inside of the crown band with two parallel strips of copper tape. Connect LEDs all along the copper strips. Slide the long legs under one strip and the short legs under the other strip.

4. Connect one end of each copper strip to the button battery. One strip should touch the positive (+) side. The other strip should touch the negative (-) side. The LEDs will light up.

5. Loop the crown band into a circle. Hot glue in place to complete the crown.

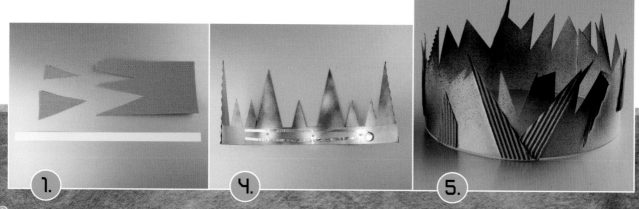

1.　4.　5.

CHANGE IT UP!

These party crowns can be made to match just about any theme. Use jewels and sticks to create a medieval vibe. Or decorate your crowns with seashells and driftwood lights for a beach party theme. You can even use simple button battery circuits to make magical, glowing seashells as party favors!

SALT AND DOUGH CIRCUITS

Just like graphite and copper, salt is a great conductor. When made into dough, you can make circuits with it. You can buy conductive dough in craft stores or you can make your own.

CONDUCTIVE DOUGH

WHAT YOU NEED

1 ½ cups (210 grams) flour, plus extra
   for dusting
1 cup (240 milliliters) water
¼ cup (48 g) salt
½ cup (120 mL) lemon juice
1 tablespoon (15 mL) vegetable oil
food coloring
saucepan
wooden spoon
cutting board

1.

3.

1. Set aside ½ cup (70 g) of flour. Mix the other 1 cup (140 g) of flour, water, salt, lemon juice, vegetable oil, and food coloring together in the saucepan.

2. Place the pan on the stove. Heat it on medium, stirring constantly.

3. Keep stirring. The mixture will start to get thicker. Stir until it forms a ball.

4. Dust a cutting board with flour. Remove the dough from the saucepan and place it on the cutting board.

5. Dust more flour on top of the dough ball. Flatten the ball with your spoon. Let cool at least five minutes.

6. Start kneading the ½ cup (70 g) of flour into the dough ball. Keep kneading until the dough is smooth and not sticky.

7. After the conductive dough cools, store it in a plastic bag for up to one week.

5.

6.

INSULATING DOUGH

WHAT YOU NEED

1 ½ cups (210 g) flour, plus extra for dusting
½ cup (95 g) sugar
3 tablespoons (45 mL) vegetable oil
½ cup (120 mL) water
food coloring
mixing bowl
wooden spoon
cutting board

MAKE IT!

1. Set aside ½ cup (70 g) of flour. Pour the other 1 cup (140 g) of flour, sugar, and vegetable oil in a bowl and mix together.

2. Add food coloring to the water. Pour little amounts of water into the bowl and mix. Repeat until the dough forms a ball.

3. Dust a cutting board with flour. Place the dough ball on the cutting board.

4. Sprinkle more flour on top of the dough. Knead the dough until it is smooth and no longer sticky.

5. Store your insulating dough in a plastic bag for up to one week.

1.

2.

WHAT YOU NEED

conductive dough
LED
9-volt battery in holder with lead wires

MAKE IT! ●●●●●●

1. Form two shapes, such as stars, out of conductive dough. Set them side by side without touching.

2. Stick the red wire from the battery holder into one dough shape. Stick the black wire into the other dough shape.

3. Open the legs of an LED. Stick the long leg into the dough with the red wire. Stick the short leg into the dough with the black wire. The LED will light up!

TIP!

If you don't want gaps between your conductive dough—or you need to layer it—place insulating dough between the conductive dough to allow the circuit to work.

GLOWING DOUGH CAMP SCENE

Conductive dough can be shaped into all sorts of glowing art projects. See for yourself with a project that brings back fond camping memories.

WHAT YOU NEED

conductive dough
insulating dough
LEDs
2 9-volt batteries with holders and leads

MAKE IT!

1. Form campfire logs out of conductive dough.

2. Make orange and yellow flames out of conductive dough.

3. Make a fire ring out of insulated dough. Place the logs and the flames on the fire ring to look like a campfire. Be sure to leave a small gap between the fire and the logs.

4. Stick the red wire from the battery holder into the dough flame. Stick the black wire from the battery holder into the dough wood.

5. Open the legs of the LEDs. Stick the long legs into the dough flame, and stick the short legs into the dough wood. The bulb will light and give your campfire a glow.

6. Make a simple triangle-shaped tent out of dough. Use conductive dough for the sides of the tent. Connect a line of insulated dough along the top of the tent to hold the two sides together. Then follow steps 4 and 5 to connect an LED, like a lantern, to the inside of the tent.

1.

2.

4.

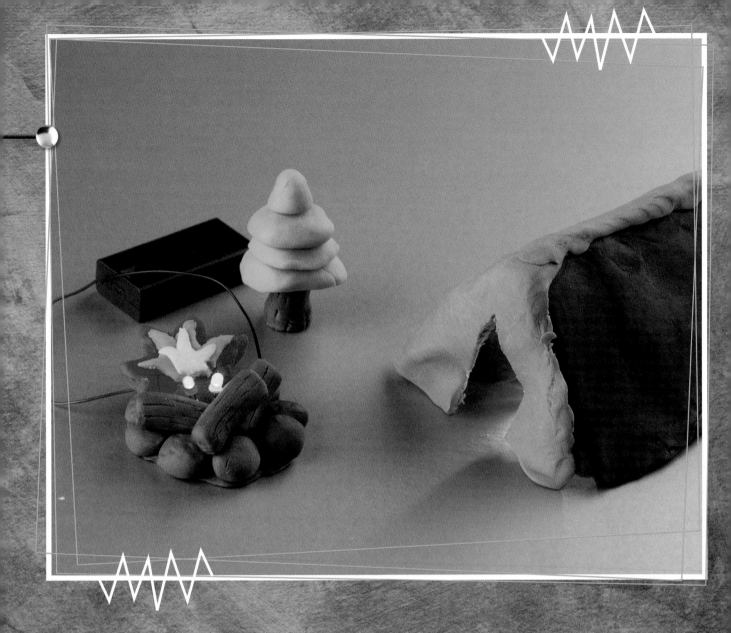

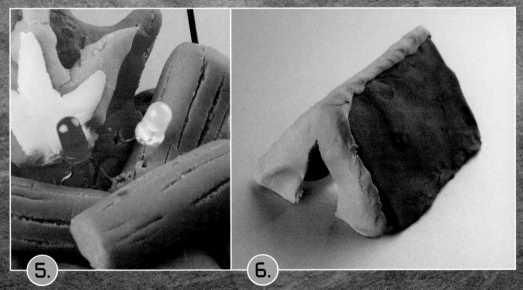

5.

6.

MOVING CIRCUITS

Now that you can connect simple circuits, let's make circuits that move! Batteries store energy for use when you need it. Magnets can be used to make electricity. They can work independently or together in the circuits you create.

WHAT YOU NEED

low-speed hobby motor
AA batteries in holder with switches
    and lead wires
mini vibrating motor
CR2032 button battery
neodymium magnets
AA battery
copper wire
needle-nose pliers

MAKE IT! ●●●●○

POWER A MOTOR

1. Connect the black wire from the battery holder to the red wire from the motor. Then connect the remaining two wires the same way.

2. Wrap and secure both connections with electrical tape.

3. Switch on the battery pack and watch the shaft on the motor spin!

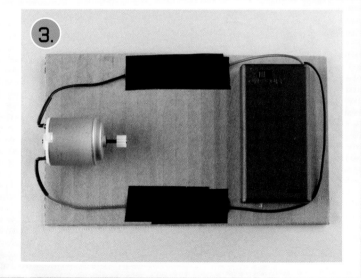
3.

CONNECT A MINI VIBRATING MOTOR

1. Connect the black wire from the mini vibrating motor to the negative (-) side of the button battery. Secure the connection with electrical tape.

2. Connect the red wire from the motor to the positive (+) side of the battery. Watch the motor wiggle!

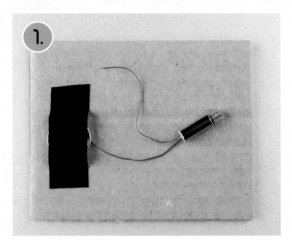

MAKE A HOMOPOLAR MOTOR

1. Stack the neodymium magnets on top of each other.

2. Set the AA battery on top of the magnets, positive (+) side down.

3. Wrap the copper wire down around the battery to make a coil. The coil should be loose around the battery and magnet stack.

4. Use a needle-nose pliers to bend a small dip at the top of your wire coil.

5. Balance the dip on top of the battery and watch the wire coil spin!

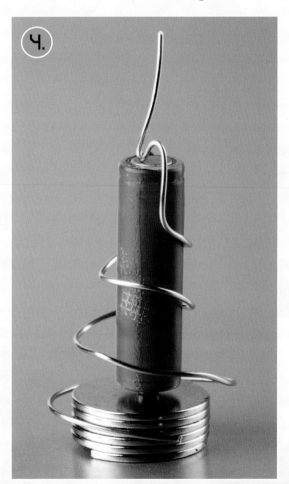

ANIMATED ART BOTS

Have a little fun by building an animated art bot. Its whacky wiggling will have you giggling!

WHAT YOU NEED

mini vibrating motor
CR2032 button battery
electrical tape
jar lid
hot glue gun
soup can
miscellaneous craft materials

MAKE IT!

1. Connect the red wire from the vibrating motor to the positive (+) side of the button battery.

2. Connect the black wire from the vibrating motor to the negative (-) side of the battery. The motor will wiggle!

3. Secure the circuit to the underside of the jar lid with electrical tape. Then disconnect one wire from the circuit while you build the rest of the project.

4. Hot glue the soup can to the top of the jar lid.

5. Decorate the can with miscellaneous craft materials. Be creative and have fun giving your art bot some personality.

6. Reconnect the wires under the jar lid to start the vibrating motor. Set the art bot on a table and watch it wiggle!

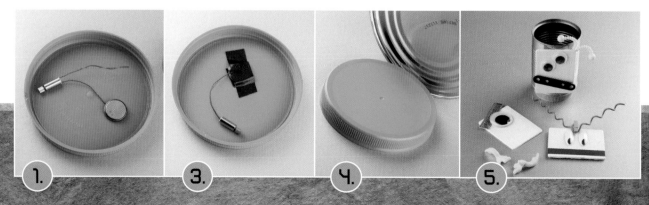

1.   3.   4.   5.

TIP!

When your art bot isn't in motion, use it as a storage container. It is perfect for holding brushes, art pencils, or circuit making tools.

SPINNING WIRE ART

Bend it, shape it, and then give it a spin!
This whirling wire art is guaranteed to wow!

WHAT YOU NEED

copper wire
needle-nose pliers
round cardboard box with removable lid
awl
cardboard
hot glue gun
small wood block
motor with lead wires
propeller
AA batteries in holder with lead wires
electrical tape

MAKE IT!

1. Bend the copper wire into a country or state shape. Make sure to leave extra wire on each end. Use a needle-nose pliers to help you bend the wire.

2. Use an awl to poke two holes in the bottom of the cardboard box. Slide the two ends of the wire shape into the holes so it stands up.

3. Cut out a cardboard circle slightly larger than the box. Glue the box with the wire shape to the cardboard circle. Set aside.

4. Glue a small block of wood to the center of the box's lid. Then glue the motor to the wood block.

5. Slide a propeller onto the motor shaft.

6. Glue the cardboard circle on top of the propeller.

7. Connect the red wire from the motor to the black wire on the battery holder. Then connect the remaining two wires. Wrap the connections in electrical tape.

8. Turn the motor on and watch your wire art spin.

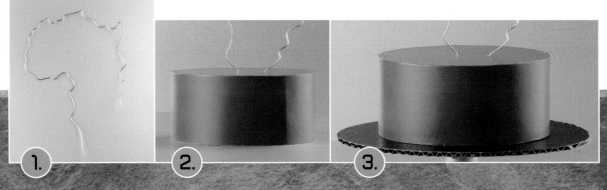

GIRAFFE DIORAMA

Take your dioramas from dull to delightful with the magic of motion. It's time to get set for a circuit safari!

WHAT YOU NEED

needle-nose pliers
copper wire
AA battery
3 to 4 neodymium magnets
cardboard box
craft grass
toy trees

MAKE IT!

1. Stack the neodymium magnets on top of each other. Set the battery on top of the magnet stack, negative (-) side down.

2. Use a needle-nose pliers to bend a piece of copper wire into the shape of a giraffe's head. Bend a small dip at the bottom of your wire shape.

3. Wrap the rest of the wire around the battery to make a coil. The coil should be loose around the battery.

4. Balance the dip on top of the battery. Watch your wire shape spin!

5. Paint a cardboard box and decorate it with craft grass or toy trees. Place the spinning giraffe inside the box to complete your diorama.

TIP!

If your wire shape doesn't spin or balance right away, just keep adjusting the wire until it spins quickly.

1.   2.   4.   5.

CHANGE IT UP!

Flip your battery over and put the positive side (+) on top of the magnet. What happens? Which direction does it spin? The shape will turn the opposite direction.

BE CAREFUL!

Neodymium magnets can be found online. They're very strong, so be careful using them. They will break or shatter if you let them snap together. If you have a pacemaker or other health device, use caution or avoid doing projects with neodymium magnets.

GLOSSARY

animated (AN-i-may-tid)—lively

battery (BA-tuh-ree)—a container holding chemicals that store and create electricity

button battery (BUHT-uhn BA-tuh-ree)—a small, disc-shaped battery

centerpiece (SEN-tur-pees)—a decorative object at the center of a table

component (kuhm-POH-nuhnt)—a part of a machine or system

conductor (kuhn-DUHK-tuhr)—a material that lets heat, electricity, or sound travel easily through it

controller (kuhn-TROHL-uhr)—a switch or other mechanism in a circuit that starts and stops the flow of electricity

current (KUHR-uhnt)—a flow of electrons through an object

diorama (dy-uh-RA-muh)—a three-dimensional replication of a scene, often in miniature

engineering (en-juh-NEER-ing)—using science to design and build things

graphite (GRAF-ite)—a black or gray mineral in pencils; graphite is the part of a pencil used for writing

insulator (IN-suh-lay-tur)—material that does not allow electricity to flow through

LED (EL-EE-DEE)—a type of light; LED stands for light-emitting diode

load (LOHD)—a device to which power is delivered

magnet (MAG-nit)—a piece of metal that attracts iron or steel

neodymium magnet (nee-oh-DIME-ee-um MAG-nit)—a very strong, permanent magnet made up of the elements neodymium, iron, and boron

origami (or-uh-GAH-mee)—the Japanese art of paper folding

switch (SWICH)—the part of a circuit that turns electrical objects on or off; a switch creates a gap in a circuit

READN MORE

Nydal Dahl, Oyvind. *A Beginner's Guide to Circuits: Nine Simple Projects with Lights, Sounds, and More!* San Francisco: No Starch Press, 2018.

Olson, Elsie. *Connect It! Circuits You Can Squish, Bend, and Twist.* Cool Makerspace Gadgets and Gizmos. Minneapolis: Abdo, 2018.

Roland, James. *How Circuits Work.* Connect with Electricity. Minneapolis: Lerner, 2017.

INTERNET SITES

DK Find Out: Circuits
https://www.dkfindout.com/us/science/electricity/circuits

Left Brain, Craft Brain: Circuit Activities for Kids
https://leftbraincraftbrain.com/circuit-activities-kids

Science Games for Kids: Electricity Circuits
http://www.sciencekids.co.nz/gamesactivities/electricitycircuits.html

A **4D** BOOK

MAKE **ART** WITH **CIRCUITS**

BY CHRIS HARBO
AND SARAH L. SCHUETTE

A **4D** BOOK

MAKE **CIRCUITS** YOU CAN **WEAR**

BY CHRIS HARBO
AND SARAH L. SCHUETTE

A **4D** BOOK

MAKE **CIRCUITS** THAT **GLOW** OR **GO**

BY CHRIS HARBO
AND SARAH L. SCHUETTE

A **4D** BOOK

MAKE **GAMES** WITH **CIRCUITS**

BY CHRIS HARBO
AND SARAH L. SCHUETTE